BIRD WATCHING FOR CATS

AN ENTERTAINMENT GUIDE FOR INDOOR FELINES

BY KIT AND GEORGE HARRISON

BIRD WATCHING FOR CATS

AN ENTERTAINMENT GUIDE FOR INDOOR FELINES

BY KIT AND GEORGE HARRISON

WILLOW CREEK PRESS

Minocqua, Wisconsin

All photographs featured in *Bird Watching for Cats* are © George H.
Harrison, with the exception of the following:
Ron Kimball, page 2 (cat) and cover; Louisa Preston, pages 5 and 6; Kent
and Donna Dannen, page 24; and Hazel Schmeiser / Unicorn Stock, page
80

Published by Willow Creek Press
P.O. Box 147
Minocqua, Wisconsin 54548

Designed by Heather M. McElwain

For information on other Willow Creek Press titles,
call 1-800-850-9453

Library of Congress Cataloging-in-Publication Data
Harrison, Kit.
    Bird watching for cats : an entertainment guide for indoor felines / by
Kit and George Harrison.
        p.   cm.
    ISBN 1-57223-189-0
    1. Games for cats. 2. Bird watching. I. Harrison, George H. II.
Title.
SF446.7.H37   1998
636.8--dc21   98-30020
                                         CIP

Printed in Canada

TABLE OF CONTENTS

FOREWORD

One of the great joys in our lives is the endless pageant of wild birds at the feeders and water areas outside our windows. Another is our cat, Amy, and before her, Patti, then Purr, Taji, Romeo, and so on.

Some fellow bird watchers are horrified that we are cat owners, believing that the two must be mutually exclusive. Nothing could be further from the truth. The reason is simple: our cats have never set paw outside (except in a carrier for car travel), yet they have been content, well-adjusted kitties that have enjoyed watching birds as much as we have.

You may have had the opportunity at some point to see a cat's reaction to the sight of a wild bird outside. When the bird is first spotted, the cat's head bobs up instantly to verify the sighting. Then, she may run at full speed — but low to the ground — to get closer. On the final approach, she is stalking a step at a time, crouching in a pre-pounce position. If the bird is still in view when she gets to the window, she starts rapidly chattering, *"Eh, eh, eh, eh, eh,"* at the same time mesmerized by the creature on the other side of the glass. When the bird flies, her muscles tense, following the movement with her eyes, until the object of her excitement is out of sight. Now that's entertainment . . . for both of you!

— *Kit and George Harrison*
Hubertus, Wisconsin

ACKNOWLEDGMENTS

During the course of producing this book, we had the delightful experience of working with numerous cats on two continents. We want to thank those cats and their owners for helping us write and illustrate *Bird Watching for Cats*.

Thanks to Catherine Althaus and her two bright-eyed black panthers, Nedd and Ben (left), who live in London, England; and to John and Joy Haig and the dignified Sir Thomas Plushpaws, who live in Gloucestershire, England.

In America, we had the pleasure of working with Stormy, the gentlemanly red Persian who shares the home of Peter, Kim and Jennifer Harrison; Sidney and Amy, the avid feline bird watchers that specialize in hummingbird watching at Ardie and Nancy Zimmer's kitchen window; Missy, Joyce Dettmers' sprightly, slightly cross-eyed, highly sociable Siamese; Nikki, the fluffy white senior citizen and her younger, colorful colleague Dexter, owned by Robert and Jennifer Kopp; the sleek, black, and playful Amy and Onyx, companions of Gerald and Cindy Ponko; Virginia Harrison's Maxi, the dainty Burmese, and her associate Poci, the charming foundling; and Poci's grown-up son, Hope, who was adopted by Lisa Dillenburg; two cats of unknown names and ownerships in the Florida Keys; and our own beloved white Persian bird watcher, Amy Wheezer-cat.

INTRODUCTION

Sharing your life with an indoor cat means that the house never feels empty when you return. You are greeted with a feline caress as your cat rubs against your leg, inviting you to stroke her or pick her up for a cuddle. When you've settled down, she is there on your lap, soothing you with her contented purring.

No matter how long you have lived together, your cat remains mysterious, affectionate, adorable, maddeningly independent, inscrutable, and each cat, in its own unique way, utterly irreplaceable.

Keeping Thomas or Thomasina safely indoors is one of the things you can do to offer him or her an excellent chance for a longer and healthier life. If there is any negative aspect to keeping a cat indoors it is that for some cats, boredom may set in, especially for those who are left alone for hours at a stretch, as when their owners are at work. You can easily cure the ennui by providing them with entertainment that is safe and natural — and it could lead to a new dimension in your life, too. Offer them the excitement of watching wild birds.

We know that cats are by nature dedicated bird watchers that can be entertained, indeed dazzled, by the sight of birds all day long.

Cats that spend their lives indoors, separated from their feathered quarries by a pane of window glass, will still be able to satisfy their hunting and stalking instincts . . . but without killing, injuring, or traumatizing the birds on the other side.

To the contrary, the birds also benefit from this arrangement when you, as a cat owner, cater to the birds' needs while supplying endless hours of amusement for your house-bound pet.

CREATE A BIRD SANCTUARY FOR INDOOR CATS

The Goal: Ginger sits at her favorite window chattering excitedly, eyes glued to the small cedar a few inches beyond the glass, tail swishing back and forth. In the cedar, a female robin stands at the edge of the deep cup nest in which her four babies are all stretching their necks to be fed. Bird watching for cats at its finest!

Birds may be abundant in your neighborhood, even if you've never taken note of them. But from your cat's point of view, indoors looking out, those birds are too far away to be of interest. The solution? Bring the birds closer by creating an attractive natural habitat for them just outside the best viewing windows of your home or apartment, so the birds will come to the windows where your kitty can see them up close and personal.

Certain types of cover can also offer nesting sites for the birds your cat watches. After recognizing that the cat on the other side of the window is not a danger, a bird may feel secure enough to build its nest and raise its young within inches of you and your pet. Dense shrubs, like this arbor vitae (left and right), planted just outside a window, can offer ideal nesting for a variety of songbirds, including robins.

Select the Best Bird Windows

Begin by taking a tour of your home or apartment and taking note of which windows have the best views of your backyard or garden. Imagine you and your cat watching lovely and lively songbirds through

Missy (above) waits eagerly for one of the birds that frequents the stick-on mealworm feeder, while Thomas (right) keeps an eye on a peanut feeder.

those windows, so close that you'll be able to see each feather, the sharpness of the birds' bills, their delicate legs, and their sparkling dark eyes.

Windows or patio doors on the ground floor or overlooking a balcony usually work best. Though one window is sufficient, two or three windows, or a patio door, are even better, and should make bird watching even more exciting for your feline. Glass patio doors are especially good, because it's likely that if you already have them, your cat is used to sitting there and looking out. In any case, the windows or doors you choose will be places in which your four-legged bird watcher will feel most comfortable watching birds, and at which the birds will feel most comfortable while they are eating, bathing, or nesting.

You'll also want those windows to have enough space around them on the outside for some flowers, small shrubs or small trees. You don't need space for a whole garden, just enough to plant up to three key items of vegetation. If the bird window or patio door looks out onto a balcony, the balcony should have enough space for the placement of hanging or potted vegetation.

What to Plant

To be successful in attracting birds outside your cat's viewing windows, you'll need to provide the birds with the kinds of natural vegetation in which they will feel at ease. These plants are called "cover," because they give the birds the protective cover they need for escape, should they be threatened by a predator such as a hawk, owl, or, dare we say it . . . a free-roaming house cat. Unless birds see sufficient protective cover around the windows, they simply will not visit them, no matter how much food and water is offered.

The best kinds of cover plants will vary by geographic region, as well as by the size and location of the windows. In the eastern and midwestern United States, for example, windows can be enhanced with a small cedar, spruce, or yew a few inches to the right or left of the window, planted either in the soil or in a pot, to offer dense cover throughout all four seasons. The addition of a highbush cranberry would give excellent cover throughout the warm seasons, and yield red berries that some birds use as food

With potted shrubs and stick-on feeders, a successful bird watching window for your cat can be achieved almost instantly. Amy spends hours in this bay window, where there's always some bird activity to catch her eye.

during the cold seasons. A spring planting of geraniums, fuchsias or impatiens, also located close to the glass, in the soil or in hanging or standing pots, would provide additional cover, while offering red, orange or pink nectar flowers to hungry hummingbirds. (See chart for plants that are appropriate for each region of the country on page 21.)

When arranging the vegetation, keep in mind that all cover plants must be small enough and situated in such a way that they do not block the view through the windows for your cat. They should be placed near enough to the glass to provide effective protection for birds, yet with enough room remaining around the window for the placement of feeders, and/or a birdbath, and/or a birdhouse.

Hummingbirds love to sip nectar at fuchsias (top) and other colorful hanging plants, while the fruit of highbush cranberry (bottom) is enjoyed by thrushes, waxwings, cardinals, mockingbirds, and many more.

COVER FOR BIRD-WATCHING CATS

	TALL TREES	SMALL TREES	TALL SHRUBS	LOW SHRUBS	PLANTS & FLOWERS
NORTHEAST	White pine Hemlock Colorado spruce Sugar maple White and red oak Beech Birch	Flowering dogwood Crabapple Hawthorn Cherry Serviceberry Red cedar	Sumac Dogwood Highbush cranberry Elderberry Everbloom honeysuckle Winterberry Autumn olive Wisteria	Blackberry Blueberry Summer sweet Red osier dogwood Huckleberry	Panic grass Timothy Hosta Sunflower
SOUTHEAST	Longleaf pine Loblolly pine Shortleaf pine Ash Beech Walnut Live oak Southern red oak Black gum Pecan Hackberry	Holly Dogwood Serviceberry Cherry Persimmon Red cedar Palmetto Hawthorn Crabapple	Sumac Dogwood Elderberry	Blackberry Blueberry Bayberry Spicebush Huckleberry	Panicgrass Sunflower
NORTHWEST	Douglas fir Ponderosa pine Western white pine Lodgepole pine Colorado spruce Oregon white oak California black oak Bigleaf maple	Hawthorn Serviceberry Dogwood	Sumac Bitterbrush Russian olive Elderberry Buckthorn Madrone	Blackberry Blueberry Snowberry Oregon grape	Turkeymullein Timothy Sunflower Filaree Lupine Fiddlenecks Tarweed
SOUTHWEST	Arizona cypress Piñon pine Live oak Bitter cherry	Serviceberrry Dogwood Mesquite Crabapple	Mulberry Lote bush Sumac Manzanita Madrone	Utah juniper Blackberry Spicebush Prickly pear Algerita	Turkeymullein Sunflower Filaree Lupine Fiddlenecks

How and When to Plant the Cover

There are three options for planting window cover: In the soil beneath the windows; in containers that are positioned under or next to the windows (either on the ground or in window boxes); or hanging from above the windows. Though planting the cover directly in the soil may or may not give a better appearance from outside the house, we believe potted plants have more advantages. By planting or purchasing cover plants in pots, the flowers, small shrubs and small trees are always portable, can be moved to other windows, rearranged at any window to suit the requirements of the season and the birds, and can easily be retired if the vegetation grows too large for use at the windows.

The best time for planting trees and shrubs in the ground outside your cat's bird-watching windows is spring or fall, the same as it would be if you were to plant them in any other part of your backyard. And, as with any other newly planted trees or shrubs, you'll want to keep them well watered. If you opt for potted trees or shrubs, they can be installed at any time of the year.

Spring is obviously the best season for planting or placing flowers and flowering vines for hummingbirds, those tiny feathered jewels that will delight any bird-watching cat.

Cover may be planted in the ground, in hanging pots, or in containers on the ground outside the window or door.

Nesting Sites in the Cover

W hile the cover you plant is primarily intended as shelter for the birds that will visit the window feeders and baths, it may also serve as a nesting area for cardinals, robins, chipping sparrows, house finches or mockingbirds. These birds typically seek dense shrubbery in which to hide their nests, and the dense cover next to your windows may appeal to them. House finches are renowned for nesting in hanging baskets of geraniums, impatiens and fuchsias. If birds build nests in any of your window cover plants, you and your cat can monitor the whole nesting process, from the first twig carried to the nest to the moment when the last fledgling pops out of the nest on its maiden flight. A captivating sight for your cat!

Sidney (right) is held up to the window by his owner for a brief peek at a nest full of baby robins while the mother bird is temporarily away.

Other Kinds of Natural Cover

There are other forms of natural cover that can give birds the security they require while visiting your cat's viewing windows. Your natural Christmas tree, for example, can easily be retired to the outside of a window and lashed or staked to keep it from falling or being blown away (see "Bird Christmas Trees" on page 73). Also, brush piles or sheaves, made from the trimmings of trees and shrubs, make excellent bird cover and may be arranged outside a bird-watching window in a pleasing manner that will be acceptable to you, the birds, and the feline observer.

Recommendations for Beginners

Initially, a potted shrub and a hanging pot overflowing with impatiens or geranium ivy may be enough cover for a standard window. Outside a patio door, at least two shrubs should be available to the birds, placed as close to the feeders as possible without obstructing your cat's view of the action. Continue adding vegetation over time. The more natural it looks to the birds, the more they'll like it. The more they like it, the more your cat will be entertained by their presence.

BIRD FEEDERS FOR CATS TO WATCH

The Goal: Sylvester crouches at the patio door, spellbound, his nose twitching a few inches from the glass, his tail thrashing from side to side, little chattering noises revealing his excitement. Outside, a small flock of goldfinches contentedly eat cracked sunflower seeds and twitter to each other with canarylike notes, their brilliant yellow plumages glowing in the sunshine.

A mong the many enticements that bring wild birds close to windows for Sylvester and his fellow indoor felines to watch, a bird feeder filled with appropriate foods and surrounded by natural cover will probably be the most successful.

There are myriad bird feeders, as many or more types of bird foods as there are cat foods, and a variety of ways to position them at windows. Some feeders and foods may appeal to specific kinds of birds. A few feeders and foods appeal to many kinds of birds, and those are the ones with which you should begin as you are getting your cat's bird windows set up.

Stormy (left) is captivated by the animated goldfinches. Whatever style of feeder you choose, it should be located close to the window so that you and your cat will be aware of all the activity it brings.

The Best Window Feeders

There have been some resourceful innovations in window bird feeders, resulting in an impressive selection that attach to the window pane, drawing in the birds to pointblank range. Most of these window feeders use plastic suction cups to hold the feeders in place against the glass.

Some of the stick-ons are small, square, tray feeders, with mesh floors for good drainage to keep the food dry, and room for several birds to eat at the same time. Some birds, including cardinals and blue jays, prefer flat surfaces

Chickadees (above) are often the first to discover a new feeder, like one attached directly to a window. Then, other species, like the red-winged blackbird (right) will shortly join in.

on which to perch while they eat, such as these tray-type feeders provide.

There are also stick-on square single-cup, double-cup and triple-cup holders on which the cups are removable for filling and cleaning. These work well for small birds such as sparrows, juncos, chickadees and bluebirds.

And, there are even stick-on hooks that are strong enough to hold small hanging tube feeders that offer multiple perches. Filled with seed, the tube feeders are favorites of the finches, which seem to enjoy holding on tightly to small perches while the breezes sway the feeders back and forth. Finches are also quite animated, offering delightful entertainment for the cat on the other side of the window.

Hummingbird and oriole feeders, for offering sugar water, are also available in the suction-cup format. Some — for hummingbirds only — are designed with feeding ports in the tops. Others are reservoir feeders with a feeding tube or ports near the bottom. Either type can be hung from window hooks.

There are additional options for feeders, however, aside from the stick-on types. Post feeders, for example, can be established just outside the window, as long as a post can be driven into the ground or set in a stand. Any of a host

of feeders — tray, tube, or box — can then be mounted on the post. Posts specifically designed for use with bird feeders are available at wild bird stores, garden centers, or any place that sells bird feeders.

Hanging feeders are another option, hung by a chain, wire, or rope from a rain gutter, eaves, or the ceiling of a balcony. The only problem that might arise from this setup occurs if it is so close to the glass that a high wind could blow the feeder into the window, possibly damaging the glass and/or the feeder. You'll want to keep this in mind when selecting the size of the feeder and its distance from the window.

Included in the range of hanging feeders are those designed to hold suet cakes, treats sought by woodpeckers, chickadees, jays, nuthatches and others. The best suet feeders are box-shaped, made of coated heavy wire, with a hinged top for easy refilling.

Another possibility is available in the gastronomic array you can display outside your cat's bird window. You can make or buy one of the various apparatuses on which orange halves can be presented for attracting the brilliant orange-and-black orioles. These are usually hanging devices that you would hook over a rain gutter above the windows or hang from a hook beneath the eaves.

As far as Sylvester is concerned, he'll happily take his bird watching at whatever feeder you select, as long as it attracts lots of birds!

The constant motion of birds flying to and from feeders, sipping nectar, or cracking seeds, provides hours of entertainment. Sidney (left) watches hummingbirds, while Amy (above) studies goldfinches.

Best Foods For Window Bird Feeders

Seeds

The best all-around bird food, the one that appeals to the most songbird species under most conditions, is sunflower seed. It can be purchased at wild bird specialty stores or at lawn and garden centers in bags containing black oil sunflower seed (in the shell), or cracked or hulled sunflower seed (medium grain out of the shell). Both kinds are favorites of cardinals, jays, finches, chickadees, titmice, nuthatches, and even some species of woodpeckers. Sunflower seeds can be placed in tray feeders, tube feeders, or cup feeders. They are probably the best seeds for luring birds to your kitty's viewing windows.

Another excellent bird seed is niger, sometimes called thistle seed, a tiny, glossy black oil seed that is highly sought by finches. Niger may be placed in a cup feeder or in a tray feeder that has a fine mesh bottom, but it really is best in a niger seed tube feeder that has tiny feeding ports drilled specifically for that size seed.

Cracked corn is likely to attract doves, juncos, and many types of sparrows. Try it on a tray-style feeder.

A more specialized but popular seed for cardinals, grosbeaks, chickadees, and nuthatches is safflower seed, a

Two of the most popular foods for birds that will come to your feeders are sunflower seeds (left) and niger seed (above), often called thistle seed.

Having spotted a blue jay (top right) fly from the feeder, Stormy leaps onto his favorite watching spot. The chickadee (top left) and cardinal (right) are popular birds that are easy to attract to seed feeders.

medium-sized pure white seed that seems to pack a big punch for the birds that eat it.

The so-called wild bird mixes are popular grocery store items that are meant to appeal to a great variety of birds, but are actually not the best food to offer at window feeders. They often contain some filler seeds that are not eaten, and they may attract what most people consider to be less desirable birds, such as starlings or house sparrows. In the eyes of your bird-watching cat, however, all birds are equal. He will be every bit as excited by the sight of a house sparrow as he will be by that of a brilliant red cardinal.

Some birds, such as cardinals and grosbeaks, will sit on the feeder as they open and eat each seed. Blue jays are likely to quickly gulp down several seeds, hulls and all, before flying off. A chickadee selects a seed, grasps it with its feet, and

then hammers the seed with its bill to open it. It may fly to a favorite nearby perch to accomplish this, but often the chickadee will stay right at the feeder, its tap-tap-tapping announcing its presence to you and your cat. Nuthatches like to pick up seeds in their bills, fly to the trunk of a tree, and wedge the seeds into the bark, where they peck them to get to the meat inside . . . all the while clinging upside-down to the bark. The colorful finches, on the other hand, settle down for lengthy meals right on the feeder.

In various parts of the country, a male rose-breasted grosbeak (left), a female cardinal (above) or male painted bunting (right) may stop in for a snack at a seed feeder.

Suet

Woodpeckers, flickers, chickadees, titmice, nuthatches and others will eagerly dine at a suet feeder, much to your cat's delight. These birds cling to the feeder while pecking off small bits of suet through the openings in the feeder. The woodpeckers are particularly striking birds, and characteristically use their tails as a support. With their two feet and their tail, they have a handy tripod on which to securely balance themselves.

You might be able to find a butcher who can still supply you with suet, but this is a vanishing commodity that's getting harder to find as each year passes. To supply the demand, bird food companies now produce suet cakes for wild birds, and they have created more varieties than we can name here, most of them probably intended to appeal to the human purchaser more than to the avian consumer. Some are flavored (orange, for example), and many have seeds or peanut butter mixed with the suet, but the ones that we use are plain suet cakes with nothing added. They are available at most wild bird specialty stores.

Woodpeckers, such as this downy woodpecker (left) and red-bellied woodpecker (right), love suet, and will be regular visitors to the suet feeder once they discover it. Nuthatches, chickadees and titmice are suet eaters, too.

Other bird foods

Bluebirds, and now many other kinds of birds, are gobbling up mealworms from bird feeders everywhere. Mealworms used to be available only in bait shops for fishermen, but now they can be purchased at wild bird specialty stores as well. Mealworms are clean and easy to store in the refrigerator, and once discovered, they are hot items for bringing birds close to windows. Bluebirds will often respond enthusiastically to mealworms while ignoring virtually all other feeder foods. They will bring their fledglings in for a snack of mealworms, too.

Fresh fruits and some fruit jellies are worth offering to birds at the windows. In the spring, orioles can't seem to resist orange halves, and some of them love grape jelly and orange marmalade. Once the orioles discover oranges or jelly, they often decide to spend the summer nearby.

You might also consider raisins, apples, and grapes to tempt non seed-eating birds to come within range of your cat's view, including such glamour birds as rose-breasted grosbeaks, catbirds, mockingbirds, thrashers, and tanagers. Wood thrushes, hermit thrushes, and robins, all related, have also been known to eat fruits at feeders across the country.

Mealworms offered in a small, easily accessible feeder, will be gobbled up by any bluebirds in the neighborhood—especially when they have babies to feed! Try putting out 12 to 15 mealworms two or three times a day after the bluebirds find them.

Sweet on sugar water

It's no secret that hummingbirds of all kinds, from coast to coast, are sweet on sugar water, and respond enthusiastically to the nectarlike offerings at gardens and windows everywhere. One part sugar mixed with four parts of water, boiled and cooled before serving, is the formula they adore. Some people like to add a few drops of red food coloring to the sugar water, but this really isn't necessary, because all hummingbird feeders have some red or orange on them to catch the eye of any passing hummers.

If these little birds find your sugar-water feeder, they are likely to spend the summer visiting it every few minutes, all day long. Your cat will love watching these tiny, iridescent dynamos hovering at the windows, flying backward, forward, up and down, like no other bird in the world.

Stormy has discovered that sugar water feeders can attract hovering, whirring hummingbirds (above and right) that add special excitement to a cat's bird watching. A Baltimore oriole (left) likes sugar water, too.

Raising the Birds' Comfort Level

During the time the birds are discovering your new feeding area, we recommend that you give them and your cats an added advantage. We've found that putting a piece of reflective film, such as mylar, on the inside of the window works like a one-way mirror. During the day, when it is brighter outdoors than indoors, the film will appear mirrorlike to the birds, so they will be unable to see the cat or you on the other side. The cat, on the other hand, will have a clear view of the birds, and will be able to move about without frightening them away.

After the birds are visiting regularly, it is often possible to remove the reflective film with no adverse reaction from the birds, because they will have learned to feel safe there. If they do become jumpy, simply put the film back in place.

We've tried Plexiglas panels with suction cups, available at some wild bird stores, that are designed specifically for one-way viewing at bird windows. However, our experience was that they were really too small to be adequate, even when we used two of them side by side.

Some birds are timid at first about approaching feeders close to a window in which a cat is watching their every move. One solution is to apply an easily installed, easily removable sheet of mylar (left), which acts like a one-way mirror, allowing you and your cat to see the birds, but not vice-versa. An indigo bunting (right) perches nearby.

By far the best and least expensive option is to find an auto supply shop or van customizer that has one-way reflective film in stock and is willing to sell a piece to you. It is frequently used on vehicle windows, so people can't see into a car or van from the outside. You may find it available in more than one width, so have an idea of the dimensions you want, and then ask to have a piece cut to the size you require. This material is thin, flexible, lightweight, and easy to handle. After it is cut, just roll it up, take it home, and tape it to your window or patio door.

Another option is to build a blind, or hiding place, for your cat to use. Find a sturdy box that is big enough for your cat to lounge in comfortably. Set the box on its side, so that it rests on one of its sides, with the open top facing you and the closed bottom on the far side. Then, cut two peep holes or slits in the closed bottom, one that would be at your cat's eye level when he is sitting and the other at his eye level when he is lying down. They should be at least wide enough so that he can see through them with both eyes. When the box is placed in front of the window or patio door, your little stalker will love hiding in the box, unseen from outside, and watching the birdies through the peep holes.

A decorative grape vine wreath on the outside of a door was chosen by this robin for its nesting site (left). A simple but effective hiding place from which Hope (right) can observe birds without being detected is a box that has a slit for peeking at the feathered fun outside the window.

Recommendations for Beginners

When getting started with your cat's bird-watching window, we recommend that you begin with the basics. Start with a feeder filled with sunflower seeds, either in the shell or hulled. This should give you the best chance of grabbing the attention of the resident birds in your neighborhood. Then, once you've got the birds coming in on a regular basis, and if space permits, add some of the more exotic offerings, such as oranges in the spring for orioles, hummingbird feeders in the spring and summer, and safflower seed year-round for cardinals.

Thomas (left) relaxes in his favorite window for much of the day. After eventually realizing that the cat on the inside of the house is no danger to them on the outside, many birds, like the male cardinal and male house finch (right) will not hesitate to approach the feeders.

BIRDBATHS FOR CATS TO WATCH

The Goal: From the cool comfort of the house, Smoky stares intently at the birdbath outside as a handsome male robin dips his head, then splashes water all over the feathers of his red breast and slate gray back. Smoky dodges would-be sprinkles that hit the window pane.

The focus of Smoky's backyard bird watching in summer could very well be the birdbath, where an endless line of feathered beauties bathe and drink to beat the summer heat, and to keep their feathers flightworthy. Some of the most splendid birds of summer are insect eaters that do not frequent bird feeders containing seed or sugar water, nor do they eat suet.

By setting up and maintaining fresh water ponds or pools, a home owner can attract the insect-eating birds close up that would have no other reason to appear. You can achieve the same results for your cat. By establishing a birdbath just outside his bird-watching window, he will be entertained by an enticing and beautiful new cast of feathered actors.

Dexter (left) loves to watch the constant parade of birds bathing and drinking outside his window, like the robin (above) splashing in the water.

One Birdbath Bathes All

Because of the restrictions of space at the bird window, you may decide that the best birdbath to use is the traditional garden style with a basin mounted on a pedestal. Another possibility is the type that features a water dish hung by a chain or rope from the eaves of the house, or from the overhang of the balcony above the window. Hanging birdbaths are not as stable, and may be spilled by wind or blown into the window if they are too close. That could damage the bath, the window, and startle the cat.

There is an actual window birdbath available in some wild bird stores. It's a seven-inch by one-inch-deep oval that affixes to the window with suction cups. The small size of the window birdbath restricts the kinds of birds that can bathe in it to about chickadee size, but virtually any bird visitor could drink from it. Your feline birder will have a treat watching that!

Water that moves, especially water that creates gentle splashing sounds (left) is extremely alluring to birds, and will entice them in from some distance. However, even an ordinary, traditional birdbath will be enjoyed by most backyard bird, like this cardinal (right).

Don't Drown the Birds

Birds need to be able to stand in the water and splash it onto their bodies. If the birdbath you're using is more than a couple of inches deep, add a rock that juts out of the water so that birds have a place to land and can ease their way down into the water. Also, too much water could result in the birds splashing the window. Although Smoky thinks it's great fun to see the water flying around, you don't want to have to wipe the window every time a bird takes a bath.

Too little water is not good, either. If the water level is allowed to drop below the point where the birds can reach it from the rim of the bath, they will not be able to drink, nor get into the water to bathe.

Water should be no deeper than one to two inches in at least one part of the bird bath, preferably near an edge, so that the birds feel confident wading into the water to bathe. They will, in any case, be quite happy to drink from water areas that are quite a bit deeper, provided they have a rim, a rock, or some other structure on which to stand while they drink.

Water's Noise Entices

Moving water that produces splashing or dripping sounds in a birdbath has been proven to attract more birds more often. Birds can hear the water from a great distance and are drawn to it like a magnet. It pays to add a small bubbler or dripper to the water area, so that the water moves and makes an inviting sound. There is at least one gadget that may be added to a birdbath or pond that may be used as either a dripper or as a misting device (see "Sources" on page 93).

If your bird-viewing window overlooks a patio, a deck, or a spacious balcony, you might consider installing a somewhat larger water area for the birds. A permanent recirculating pool could be built, or you could acquire one of the self-contained units with built-in pumps that are available at many lawn and garden centers and wild bird stores. These are often fabricated of simulated stone that blends with natural surroundings. They are designed to be used on the ground, are generally about 20 inches high and 18 inches wide, and have a suitably shallow, recirculating water area. All you have to do is take one home, set it in an appropriate spot, add water, and plug it in.

Clean Water Is Healthy

It is important to maintain the cleanliness of the bird-bath by changing the water frequently, and, if necessary, by occasionally washing the basin with bleach (rinsing very thoroughly), if it gets covered with algae. It is probably not healthy for birds to bathe in and drink water that has been used by other birds over a long period of time.

The flowing, falling water of a backyard pond is irresistible to resident birds, including a male cardinal (left) and a male indigo bunting (right).

Food and Drink Available Here

I f a birdbath is set up in conjunction with a bird feeder at the same bird-watching window, and surrounded by some natural habitat, feathered visitors could eat, drink and even take a bath on the same stage, all for your cat's entertainment.

Recommendations for Beginners

Set up a simple birdbath on a post that can be driven into the ground, or use a self-standing birdbath, locating it where it can easily be seen from the window. Remember to change the water regularly.

Amy (right) and Stormy (far right) are intrigued by the small but bold birds that use this window water dish.

Overleaf: Amy studies a robin that is about to have a bath in the shallow upper pool of this recirculating water area.

BIRDHOUSES FOR CATS TO WATCH

The Goal: Lying quietly on the cushioned window seat off the den, Cleo is absorbed in watching a mother house wren shove a green caterpillar down the throat of one of her six chicks inside the birdhouse attached to the window glass.

Your indoor cat's bird-watching adventures might just as well include watching a pair of house wrens raise a family in a window birdhouse. Wrens are busy little live wires, constantly in motion, making them a real favorite of bird-watching cats!

Attached to the glass on four large suction cups, the window birdhouse is a typical square wren-sized bird box with a 1¼–inch entrance hole that faces away from the window. The back panel is made of see-though Plexiglas that allows your kitty companion, and anyone else on the indoor side of the window, to see all the activity in the house.

A very special experience, though one that doesn't come easily, is the joy of having a pair of birds raise their family in a birdhouse that allows you and your kitty to watch the entire process. Poci (left) and Nedd (right) are wide-eyed at what they see.

Put Up the House Early

It is best to get the house up on the window pane sometime in early spring, so that it has a "For Rent" sign on it when the male house wrens return to backyards across the country. During the initial period of exposure, it is usually helpful to tape a piece of black paper or cardboard over the inside of the window where the house meets the glass. This will keep the wrens from being frightened by you or your cat's movements when they make their first exploratory visits inside the house.

If the male wren is interested in the mini piece of real estate you are offering, he will take an option on it by beginning to fill it with twigs even before a female arrives on the scene. If there are more wren houses nearby, he's likely to do the same with them. Once he has placed sticks into several potential nesting sites around his territory, he will escort his newly arrived bride on a tour of the housing market. She will be the one to make the final selection of where they will raise their family.

Once the birds build the nest and begin incubating eggs, they will be more attached to the nest and less skittish. At that point, you should be able to cautiously remove the cover paper for better viewing. Your cat will then be able to see the eggs hatch and check out the parents scurrying to

deliver food to the tiny chicks every few minutes through the daylight hours. As the chicks develop, their eyes open, their fuzzy down grows more apparent, they demand more food, and the space inside the house inevitably becomes filled with restless nestlings. Feathers will sprout as the youngsters near their time for fledging. All of this activity on the other side of the glass will keep your cat captivated for weeks.

Usually, a nesting bird will require plenty of nearby cover as well as minimal disturbance, especially until a few days after the babies hatch. Block off the see-through area at the back of the birdhouse and peek in only when you know the adult is temporarily out of the house. Or install a sheet of one-way mylar on the window to preserve the bird's sense of privacy.

Traditional Birdhouses

Traditional birdhouses may also be used, hung either in a nearby tree within view of the window, or mounted on a post near the window. For the best viewing, try to position the birdhouse so that the opening faces the window.

Birdhouses come in many shapes and sizes. The dimension of the opening and the site of the birdhouse often are the determining factors for the type of birds that it might attract. Bluebirds like fairly open areas, or houses in fence rows, and are unlikely to chose to nest this close to your home. Chickadees, titmice, house sparrows, and some species of wrens, however, are possible tenants for a birdhouse close to the cat's bird window.

Your cat won't be able to witness all the commotion inside these houses, but she'll see the constant comings and goings of the parents, first as the nest inside is under construction. Then, after a couple of fairly quiet weeks during which the eggs are laid, usually one per day, and then incubated when the clutch is complete, the chicks will hatch. This spurs a renewed flurry of activity, sending the frenzied parents out on incessant forays to find enough food to stuff into those hungry mouths. If you provide mealworms, many of those foraging expeditions could bring the harried parents straight to the feeder at your cat's viewing window time and again.

Recommendations for Beginners

For your first attempt, we recommend a traditional wren house mounted on a post near the viewing window. If you believe there is a good chance that you will have a robin or cardinal nesting in a shrub next to the window, or a house finch in a hanging basket of flowers, it would be best to put a reasonable space between the birdhouse and the available nesting sites of the different species.

BIRD CHRISTMAS TREES FOR CATS TO WATCH

The Goal: With her nose against the cold window pane, Fluffy watches with curiosity as a downy woodpecker partakes of the suet cake hanging on the birds' Christmas tree.

A festive way to celebrate the holiday season with your cat and the birds is to place an evergreen outside the window and decorate it with seasonal goodies for the birds to eat.

The practice of being kind to the animals during the holidays is a tradition dating back to the times of St. Francis of Assisi, who advised farmers to give their animals extra grain at Christmas. New straw was put in the stables, animals were given a rest from work, and wild birds were fed seeds and corn. For Norwegians, Christmas preparations began as soon as the harvest ended. After all the grain had been cut and bundled, the last remnants were gathered into sheaves by children and tied to the tops of long poles in the farmyard as a Christmas feast for the birds.

By carrying on the tradition at your house, you will present interesting and wholesome food for the birds, and a bounty of exciting bird watching for your indoor kitty.

Missy (left) discovers that a birds' Christmas tree is full of activity.

Recycle the Christmas Tree

Either procure a special tree or recycle the family Christmas tree for placement outside the window or near the patio door. Make sure that it is secured enough to withstand strong winds, as well as the weight of snow or of other animals that may climb it to investigate. Then, gather the decorations.

Decorating a Christmas tree for birds is fun for you, and a real treat for your bird-watching cat when the birds start to investigate the goodies. You can either move your natural Christmas tree outdoors when you've finished with it after the holidays, or decorate an evergreen that is growing next to the house outside one of the windows or patio doors where your cat spends time.

Decorations for the Birds' Christmas Tree

Garlands of Goodies

Using a strong needle and heavy-duty thread, string garlands from any combination of popped corn, fresh cranberries, red grapes, green grapes, apple pieces, chunks of plain doughnuts, and raisins. For easier stringing, allow the popped corn to sit uncovered at room temperature for a day or two before you begin. Freshly popped corn tends to crumble when the needle is inserted; allowing it to absorb a small amount of normal household humidity seems to take care of this problem. For convenience, work in lengths of 30 to 45 inches, knotting the ends to keep the fruit from slipping off. Leave a few inches of thread at each end if you wish to tie your garlands together as you drape the laden strings carefully over the tree boughs.

Suet Balls

Into a base of melted beef suet, mix cornmeal, sunflower seeds, white millet seeds and safflower seeds. When it is cool enough to handle, but not yet set, shape the mixture into balls around lengths of yarn or string that have been knotted at the bottom. Allow the balls to harden before hanging them on the tree.

Suet, either with or without seeds added, makes attractive, edible ornaments, which are especially popular with woodpeckers.

Corn Treats

Offer ears of yellow, strawberry, or Indian corn. Gather two or three ears together, then tightly tie string or yarn around the pulled-back husks, leaving extra string attached for hanging the ears on the tree.

Cup of Ash

Mountain ash berries, added to melted suet and spooned into cupcake tins to harden, make a one-dish meal for some birds.

Niger Seed Bags

Small mesh bags of niger (thistle) seeds hung from the Christmas tree will bring in the finches.

Festive Apples

Red or yellow apples, hung with string from their stems, form colorful Christmas tree balls.

Sacks of Suet

Chunks of beef suet in red mesh bags, hung from the tree boughs, do wonders for woodpeckers.

Bells, Balls and Bricks

Many wild bird stores, lawn and garden centers, and hardware stores sell small hanging bird foods during the Christmas season that will look lovely, in addition to bringing birds into the Christmas tree for your cat to watch.

The birds' Christmas tree should stay green for months, and with a little restocking of the goodies from time to time, it could remain a busy place for birds to gather, just outside the window. The tree provides its own protective cover for the birds, and with food dispersed among the branches, the birds' Christmas tree will be a point of convergence for the birds, providing entertainment for you and your cat all winter long.

Recommendations for Beginners

If you do nothing more than move your Christmas tree outdoors, securing it near one of your birding windows, you will have provided instant cover for the birds, even if you don't have the time or inclination to decorate it with bird treats.

BIRD VIDEOS AND BIRD SONGS FOR INDOOR CATS

The Goal: Sitting on top of the television, Felix peers over the front at a mourning dove on the screen. He sees the bird moving on the television, and hears its mournful call from the speakers. High-tech bird watching is great home entertainment for this lucky kitty.

To give your indoor cat an occasional change from watching birds at the window, surprise him with a bird video that features closeups of birds singing and calling as they go about their daily routines in the great outdoors.

We discovered the feline fun factor of videos during the time we were producing our own bird videos for PBS TV. When we ran the tapes on our television, our usually dignified and serene pussy cat came bounding into the room, attracted by the sounds of the birds. Her eyes locked onto the orioles, cardinals, warblers and bluebirds as they darted across the screen. She was completely enthralled. Her excitement rising, she tried to zero in on the singing birds, examining the television from every angle, including peeking behind it.

When things are quiet at the bird-watching window, try entertaining your kitties with a bird video. They'll love it! Amy (above) finds the quick movements of birds on the television screen, as well as their songs and calls on the soundtrack, irresistible.

Our experience is not unique. In fact, there are videos on the market just for cats that will entertain even the most discerning bird-watching kitty. Some bird watching videos include a repeat of the program, minus the narration, with the soundtrack of bird songs matched with the images of the birds on the screen.

The television on which the bird videos are played should be located so that your cat has a comfortable seat or ledge on which he can luxuriate during the show. Don't be surprised, though, to see him leap onto the top of the set and peer down at the birds below, or glance behind it for the source of the bird songs.

Another way to bring outdoor birds indoors for your cat is with a tiny video camera (right) that attaches to a bird feeder, birdhouse or birdbath, transmitting both sound and image through a cable to the television set indoors (see Closed-circuit Video in "Sources" on page 94). This setup gives your pet constant monitoring of the birds visiting a feeder, birdhouse or bath that is away from the window.

Outdoor Bird Sounds Piped Indoors for Cats

Another device, called the Wing Song, delivers the peaceful sounds of birds and other natural sounds to the indoors. A wireless microphone outside transmits sounds to the receiver indoors. Both the outdoor and indoor units are attractive, unobtrusive off-white objects that would not be objectionable in the yard or home. The Wing Song is very sensitive to outdoor sounds, and transmits them vividly to the inside, bringing the outdoors in for both cat and owner.

There are also records, tapes and CDs of bird songs available in book stores and wild bird stores, most of which were recorded by the Cornell Laboratory of Ornithology. These faithfully represent the songs and calls of all North American species. When played for your indoor cat, they are another way to stimulate his interest and pique his curiosity.

Bird calls and songs are titillating to most cats. The Wing Song brings these sounds indoors for Missy (left) via a transmitter and speaker. Some cats also listen intently to audio tapes of bird calls designed to help you learn who says what.

Bird Song Clock for Telling Cat Time

T here is a clock that actually sings a different bird song every hour, on the hour, depicting the songs of the 12 birds pictured at each hour (see Novelty Items in "Sources" on page 94). The songs, recorded by the Cornell Laboratory of Ornithology, are transmitted at full volume during daylight hours, but are muted by a light sensor at night, when these birds . . . and you . . . are probably asleep. During daylight, your cat's ears will perk up each time the bird on the clock sings the time.

Recommendations for Beginners

Get a video that features a lot of bird activity and bird sounds and watch your cat's reaction! You can find bird videos at wild bird stores, or you might try a few from your local library before making a purchase.

A clock that gives a different, and fairly realistic, bird call on each hour has Hope (left) and Stormy (right) wondering, "Where's the birdie?"

Bird Videos and Bird Songs for Indoor Cats

TOYS FOR BIRD-WATCHING CATS

The Goal: After trying unsuccessfully to distract you from your reading by jumping into your lap, settling onto your reading material and nudging his purring face against your cheek, Tigger is now sitting on a nearby chair . . . staring at you. You get the hint, and as you go to the umbrella stand where you keep a half-dozen peacock and ostrich feathers (some of them a bit bedraggled by now), Tigger's tail twitches eagerly. By the time you have one of the plumes in your hand, Tigger is at your heels, ready for action.

W hen the sun goes down and the birds disappear for the night, you've probably noticed that your cat is still alert and ready for action. That's the ideal time to provide some additional bird-oriented amusement for him, pastimes that he can indulge in on his own, or play in which you can participate with him.

Once you start to look, you'll find a plethora of toys that are birdy. Your cat will especially enjoy the ones that require you and he to interact. The hands-down favorite in this category is probably a peacock feather or an ostrich plume. You can move either of these exquisitely lovely feathers slowly, quickly, or better yet, in a *slow-slow-slow-quick-quick* sequence. Waving or sliding the feather on or close to the floor in a lazy, seductive motion will be irresistible to any cat within sight of it. The fast, darting action that follows is certain to elicit an ecstatic pounce!

Maxi (left) is in pursuit of a Whirly-Bird. Cats will chase and pounce with delight on nearly any toy that has feathers.

Other interactive toys, called wand toys, often consist of a group of feathers attached by a line to a rod (see Toys in "Sources" on page 94). By holding the end of the stick, you can make the "bird" fly in smooth, undulating, or jerking patterns. These toys are almost as surefire as the peacock and ostrich feathers, and nearly all cats will jump at the "bird" as it flies past. To keep your kitty interested in the game, let him catch it occasionally before continuing.

Naturally, there are literally dozens of styles of catnip-stuffed bird-shaped toys. Usually, the simplest designs are the most effective. However, if you want to get fancy, you can even find something like a small green satin catnip-stuffed parrot with colorful bell-tipped streamers for a tail.

We also had fun with a toy that we found just before Easter. It was being sold next to Easter baskets, jelly beans, and chocolate eggs. Resembling a baby chick, the fluffy yellow bird made realistic peeping sounds when held in the hand. It never failed to draw our own furry little denizen from wherever she was in the house, animated with wide-eyed curiosity.

These are only a few suggestions. You'll find many more once you start looking and letting your imagination loose. Check your favorite pet supply shop, web site, or catalog for others, too.

SOURCES

Books

The Backyard Bird Watcher
George and Kit Harrison
Simon & Schuster

Garden Birds of America
George and Kit Harrison
Willow Creek Press

Backyard Bird Watching for Kids
George Harrison
Willow Creek Press

A Field Guide to the Birds (East or West)
Roger Tory Peterson
Houghton Mifflin Co.

Field Guide to the Birds of North America
National Geographic Society

All the Birds of North America
HarperCollins

Videos, Cameras and Monitors

George Harrison's Birds of the Backyard: Winter into Spring
Distributed by Willow Creek Press
P.O. 147 • 9931 Hwy. 70 West
Minoqua, WI 54548
(800) 850-9453

George Harrison's Spring and Summer Songbirds
Distributed by Willow Creek Press
P.O. 147 • 9931 Hwy. 70 West
Minoqua, WI 54548
(800) 850-9453

George Harrison's The Backyard Bird Watcher
Distributed by Willow Creek Press
P.O. 147 • 9931 Hwy. 70 West
Minoqua, WI 54548
(800) 850-9453

Video Catnip
HDW Enterprises
P.O. Box 418104
Sacramento, CA 95841-8104
(916) 481-CATS (Phone and Fax)
http://www.hdw-inc.com

Closed-circuit Video

VR-100 Cam Camera

Some wild bird stores stock this item; others will be happy to order it for you. Or, contact the manufacturer directly:

Video Researchers
2010 E. Hennepin Ave.
Minneapolis, MN 55413
(612) 378-2577
www.sport-cam.com

Outdoor Sounds Monitor

Wing Song

Many wild bird stores sell the Wing Song. Or, contact:
Country Line Ltd.
4543 Taylor Lane
Warrenville Heights, OH 44128
(800) 692-2656

Audio Tapes and CDs

Birding By Ear, the Eastern/Central United States
Peterson Field Guides
Houghton Mifflin

Birding By Ear, the Western United States
Peterson Field Guides
Houghton Mifflin

Toys and Novelty Items

Singing Bird Clock, by Mark Fieldstein and Associates
Available at wild bird specialty stores and many gift shops, as well as through a number of direct mail merchants.

Whirly-Bird and Mini Plume Wand Toy©
HDW Enterprises
P.O. Box 418104
Sacramento, CA 95841-8104
(916) 481-CATS (Phone and Fax)
http://www.hdw-inc.com

One-Way Windows

LLumas R-15G is automotive film used to create a one-way mirror effect on vehicle windows, and works well on home windows to prevent birds on the outside from seeing a cat or a person inside. The film comes in rolls, can be cut to size with scissors, and is easy to tape onto window glass. Ours came from Sunbuster Glass Tinting and Auto Security, Milwaukee, Wisconsin, 414-540-6585, but similar material should be available anywhere auto glass is tinted.

Feeders

You should be able to find these feeders at wild bird specialty stores and direct-mail retailers, at many lawn and garden centers, and some hardware stores. The styles and models that we recommend for use on bird-watching windows include the following:

Stick-on tray feeder — MoBi Ledge with MoBi Mesh
Stick-on feeder — The Snack Bar, Aspects Model 001